Working Together; Achieving Success

Critiquing, Marketing, Masterminds

Carol Peterson

Honor Bound Books

Typeset interior and cover in Cambria, Georgia, Schwarzwald, Papyrus, Viner Hand ITC, Kristen ITC, and Bright regular. Used with permission from Microsoft and Adobe. Cover graphics purchased from Shutterstock with license.

ISBN-13: 978-0-9977785-8-8
ISBN-10: 0-9977785-8-X

Dedication

This book is dedicated to every writer who sits alone in their office. It is written as an encouragement to work with other writers to improve the quality of their work for our awesome readers.

It is also written with thanks to my writing partners, beta readers, critique groups, writing teachers and encouragers who have believed in my writing and kept me going over the years—especially the Inksters—Pamela Turner, Deborah Underwood, Keely Parrack and Nancy Case Humphrey.

Contents

Chapter 1

Writing is a Solitary Business

Most writers are happiest sitting in the corner of their office writing. It's not that we're introverts—exactly. Wait. Yes, most of us *are* introverts.

With that in mind, often fear sets in at some point in the writing process. What if the fabulous book I am writing/have written/plan to write is only fabulous in my own mind?

We recognize the solitary life of being a writer. Ideally, then we step out into the world with courage—first into a writing community and then together—all of us fear-ridden, trembling introverts gathered as one brave, courageous, awesomely confident clan of writers—to share our work with the world.

Maybe you are not plagued by fear or questions about the quality of your work. Or maybe you have a doctorate degree in marketing and know every bookstore owner personally who is clamoring for your next three dozen books.

Whatever your background and personality, however, we writers do most of our work alone. We are nonetheless part of a community of writers. And just as other writers have mentored, encouraged and helped us become the writers we are today, we have an obligation to give back to them and other writers so that the world is made better by the words we string together.

Fear is why this book was written. Joining with other writers to help each other and to make our writing better is what this book is about.

Let's get started.

> Eventually, writers need to leave their office and step into the world. When that first step is only as far as the writing community, we can gain encouragement and confidence to share our work more enthusiastically with our eventual readers.

Part One: Making it Good

Critique Groups, Writing Partners and Beta Readers

Chapter 2

The Need for Feedback

Whether we write fiction or non-fiction, one of the problems writers face is how to take the clarity of our project that exists inside our heads and write it, so it is understood by our reader. Some of us write by the seats of our pants. Others of us write by an outline so detailed it is nearly as many pages as our finished project. But whatever our process, there's no point writing a book no one understands.

And it's best if we get that clarity on our book before it heads into publication. In other words, we need feedback on our work; not just from people who love us, like Mom who treasures everything you ever created.

We also need feedback from people who understand the craft of writing so when there's a question or issue that isn't clear, they can know why it isn't clear and can make suggestions for how to fix it.

We need other writers.

That's the beauty of critique groups.

In a critique group, each member submits a piece of writing for feedback. The writing may be a chapter, a whole book, a blog post or an idea for something larger. The other members of the group then give feedback.

Some groups only want to see manuscripts that are close to completion. They then look not just at flow and sequence but also become spell checkers and grammarians.

Other groups only want to see the manuscript as it is being written, both because each smaller part of the project is more manageable to review, and so they can give developmental help along the way.

Other groups will look at whatever someone needs help with. It might be help developing the idea before the writing even begins. Or it might be to look at the total manuscript before it is sent to a publisher.

How then do you find a critique group that fits your needs?

Often you can find a group of like-minded writers in an organization you already belong to. Are you a member of Author's Guild? Society of Children's Writers and Illustrators? A Yahoo, Facebook or Google writing forum? An established group focused on writers often has an avenue to get members into existing critique groups.

Or you can establish a new critique group yourself by inviting writers you know.

There are lots of things to consider when setting up a critique group. Often a group will morph over time as some members leave and new members join; as members expand into different genres and as the group figures out what works (and doesn't) for the personality of the group as a whole. Still, things will run more smoothly if some guidelines are set in place from the beginning.

You may be so desperate for a critique group that you invite anyone and everyone. Sometimes that will work well for you as you grow in your writing together. Often however, critique groups will run best if certain common denominators are settled on in the beginning.

Like what? Read on.

Often, we writers are so close to our work, we can't see issues clearly. Having a fresh viewpoint can make our writing better.

Chapter 3

In-Person or Online Group

When we think of critique groups, often we imagine a group of eight or ten writers sitting by a fire at a local bed and breakfast or whispering softly in the corner of the local library. But not all critique groups meet in person. The Internet has opened a variety of new ways to "meet." Here are a few of the pros and cons of in-person vs online critique groups and what things you might want to consider when deciding which to become involved in.

First, in-person critique groups may help you develop closer personal relationships. We get to know people better when we can watch their expressions, hear their voice, see the emotions in their eyes. Their personality is more understandable, and friendships develop more quickly and more deeply when you spend several hours a week or a month together.

In a similar way, in-person critiques are often clearer with immediate give and take as points are questioned and clarified. When we receive feedback from someone in person, what they have to say can be softened by their mannerisms, their voice, their smile. Similarly, their enthusiasm for a project sounds more enthusiastic when accompanied by the tone of their voice and the way they almost hop about in their seat.

Online groups have the ability for people to be more flexible with schedules. If an in-person group meets every other Wednesday at 5:30 pm, then the members must be dedicated and commit to that time every other Wednesday, remembering that other people are counting on them for feedback, help and encouragement. If there is not total commitment by each member of the group, the group has a greater likelihood of falling apart.

Online groups however allow for different schedules. Although some groups arrange for a time to meet online—on Facetime, Skype or other venue—most groups are run so that there is a submission/critique schedule but allowing members to submit and respond generally at their convenience within that overall schedule. There can still be discussion via email or another online group set up. Questions can be asked; answers given to the group as a whole, so that all people benefit from the comments of others.

Online groups also do not limit members to a specific geographical area. I have been a member of groups scattered over a state; over a nation and worldwide. Time zones and location are no longer an issue when the group is run through the Internet, because people simply participate at their own convenience.

Online groups also enable people who live in the boondocks to be part of a writing community even if his nearest neighbor geographically is 50 miles away—as long as he has an Internet connection.

In-person groups sometimes require people to think on their feet more whereas online groups allow members to read, comment, think, revise, reflect, think of more thoughts, look into ideas or resources or publishing houses related to that project. Of course, people can go home and provide additional ideas later also, but some of us tend to love the process of reading→thinking→ more thinking→adding or revising or brainstorming our critique while we're still sitting alone in the corner of our offices and before we formally write out our critique thoughts.

Some groups also run a little bit in-person and a little bit online. For example, members might submit a piece via email ahead of a meeting so other members can have a chance to read and even prepare comments. Then they meet (less frequently) in person and share thoughts along with their already printed out critiques. In those instances, more work can be accomplished at the in-person events because much of the preparation has already been done; members already have had a chance to critique; thus, the critique discussions are more productive.

Some writers are adamant that their critique group simply must meet in person. Others prefer the convenience of attending a critique group in their jammies and slippers.

I've been a member of in-person critique groups. I've also been a member of online critique groups. I have loved them all.

The first step to setting up a critique group then is to determine whether you want to meet in person or online. Part of that decision has to do with the members personalities; part of it has to do with their lifestyle.

What is the second step?

First decide whether an in-person or online group will best meet your personality, schedule and writing needs.

Chapter4

What Type of Writing Your Group Will Cover

Most writers write in more than one genre. That means a couple of things:

1. They may be members of more than one critique group.

2. They may be in one critique group that is willing to look at multiple genres.

3. They may be in one critique group for some of their writing and might write alone for other genres, taking what they learn from their critique group and applying it to other writing.

When setting up a critique group, you might survey all potential members and find out what genres they write, what genres they may write in the future, and what their specific needs are. Then decide as a group what genre(s) your group will cover.

Keep in mind, however, that the inclusion of more than one genre can be tricky. Certain genres, for example, have basic assumptions that most writers and readers of that genre understand without those having to be stated in every story. An example of genre-specific assumptions would be high fantasy, where elves are almost universally honorable, physically elegant and live long lives. Similarly, writers and readers of science fiction set in space understand the terms *warp speed*, *Class M planets* and *drop ships*. Be aware however, that if your critique group covers multiple genres, it may take a while for members who do not read that genre to get into the swing of understanding the genre and providing helpful feedback.

Similarly, if you set up a group that writes for adults, members critiquing an occasional book for children might not understand the difference between a picture book, a picture story book, an E-Z reader and an early chapter book, and therefore, their suggestions might not only be irrelevant, they might be contrary to requirements of that specific genre.

The beauty of critique groups that allow multiple genres, of course is that all of us can learn new things and grow in our understanding and skill at writing. Just as we are advised to read widely in order to learn what works well in writing, it is also helpful to read in multiple genres to understand which tools of writing are used effectively by various genres and why.

One of the things readers of historical fiction love, for example, is being placed in that setting so they can experience the history of the time. Therefore, writers of historical fiction typically write lovely detailed narrative description to explain clothing, architecture and customs of the time.

On the other hand, action/adventure novels almost never contain detailed narrative description because it slows down the pace of the story. Rather, a more common tool for the action/adventure genre is the use of tight writing, short paragraphs, short sentences, short words, which allows the reader to quickly follow the essentials of the story without slowing down the time it takes them to read.

Therefore, an understanding of what writing tools are used in each genre and why can be helpful for us even when writing in other genres.

Whether your group is dedicated to only one genre or covers many, it is helpful to have a checklist for what a person providing feedback might look at for each type of genre. For example:

1. When critiquing novels, you might have a checklist for critique members to look at: plot, setting, character development, problem, resolution, story arc, theme, etc.

2. When critiquing non-fiction, you might have a checklist for critique members to look at: chapter organization, reader demographics, purpose of the book, internal chapter consistency.

3. When critiquing children's literature, you might have a checklist based on age and genre for: word count, reading level, interest by age, theme.

Then you might ask each member to run their project through that the appropriate checklist before submitting it to the group. That may help the writer address some of the issues before it goes to the group, saving other members time and encouraging everyone to incorporate writing tools and rules consistently. Additionally, having that checklist may help other members look at that piece in a way that provides more helpful feedback.

Some groups also like to add things to their critique such as publishers who might be looking for that type of work, additional blog post topics to engage readers and marketing ideas or niche readers the author might learn more about.

Other groups strictly limit their comments to the writing itself.

One thing that can be extremely beneficial for groups which critique a novel in progress is to have the author write a short synopsis of the novel and provide each member with that synopsis before submitting their work. This does two things:

First, if a critique member understands the character's motivation, theme and plot, he can see how the author is introducing those elements and may be able to provide thoughts about pacing, when to introduce subplots or provide ideas to make the theme stronger. Having an idea of where the story is going helps a person provide a more meaningful and helpful critique.

Remember that critique groups are there to help make the writing stronger; not to simply read a story for enjoyment. Therefore, it is of no value in critiquing to keep the ending a surprise. If the author tells the group how she plans to end the story, critique members will be better able to help her get there.

Secondly, when an author is required to write a synopsis, it forces them to clarify the book. Certainly, things change during the writing, but knowing motivation, theme and plot helps keep those things in the writer's mind during the writing. The result is often less floundering and better story flow.

Once you have found a group of writers and settled on the type of writing your group will cover, you can move on to creating your group's general guidelines for how the group will operate.

> Settle on whether your group will focus on one genre or multiple genres and books, articles or short stories.

Chapter 5

General Guidelines for Critique Groups

The next step in setting up a critique group is to determine generally how the group will be run.

Mission Statement

Determine the purpose of your critique group. Think high level mission statement. It might be as simple as:

to encourage each other in our writing with the eventual goal of publication

Or:

to grow our understanding and skill in the craft of writing

Then settle on what aspects of writing your group will include. Here are a few possibilities.

- Constructive writing critiques
- Training in the craft of writing

- Encouragement
- Prayer Support
- Insights into the publishing industry
- Networking opportunities
- Marketing thoughts

Mutual Agreement

Always also obtain agreement by every member that all members will maintain a focus of the group as a place for writing. Everyone should feel free to share their work, without worrying about political, religious or genre preferences of other members. The goal is to improve the craft of writing for the members; not to push one person's belief over another's. That is true even if the belief is expressed within the writing submitted for critique.

If one member cannot critique a piece of writing solely on the craft of writing, then allow members the option to pass on a specific piece based on differing beliefs or experience.

Similarly, each member should agree to respect the privacy of other member's personal information as well as the non-disclosure of topics of writing being submitted. Certainly, no writing submitted to the group should be shared outside the group without the prior permission of the author.

When you submit to the group, it is also helpful to have a guideline saying that the member let the group know what stage of the writing process the piece is at. Each member should also state what type of feedback they are looking for on the writing—whether you are looking for general feedback on the story, character, pacing, theme or the idea in general or for copy edits.

Each member should also make sure the group knows about any pending deadline for the piece.

Of course, underlying every interaction members have with each other should be kindness, gentleness and respect. Our writing comes not only from our heads; it comes from our hearts. Our words are precious to us and all of us share our work with others, hoping they will be loved as we love them.

Remember when giving critiques that the work has been presented with hopeful-yet-tenuous trust. Do not shred the work to pieces, just because you can, or are right, or think you know how to make it better. Similarly, receive critiques, assuming the giver had your best interests in mind.

One time-tested formula for critiquing a piece is the "sandwich" critique. Begin with what is wonderful about the piece. Then move to suggestions for improvements. Finish with repeating what worked well. Often, hearing that the reader saw something good in what you wrote, can help the writer be more open to receiving suggestions on how maybe it wasn't quite perfect—yet.

Number of Members

You might think, the more the better, but that isn't always true for critique groups. Remember that most people will spend a minimum of one hour providing feedback on each submission. If you have 20 members, even if they only submit one item a month, that is a 19-hour time commitment from each other member of the group.

The bigger the group, also the more complicated the submission rules will need to be so that not every member submits in the same week with half the people needing feedback immediately.

On the other hand, too small of a group may mean your growth in writing stagnates, or there are not enough different points of view to be helpful.

I have been part of groups as small as three and as large as 12. What has worked best for me—mainly in online groups—has been to limit the number of members from five to eight. Mathematically, eight members creates an efficient submission schedule where two members submit a piece of writing each week; meaning the other members are facing a maximum number of critiquing hours of about two per week. That's doable for most people.

Remember that, even with in-person groups, there will be additional discussion about the craft of writing, publishing and marketing beyond what is involved in critiquing work. Additionally, there will likely be give-and-take about critiques for clarification, how to implement suggestions and brainstorming.

Administrator

Even if you don't want to technically have a "leader," someone should be selected as administrator or facilitator. This person will remind the group of meeting times, submission schedules and gently nudge members to follow guidelines set up by the group.

Occasionally there may be personality conflicts or even "lively" discussions that need to be addressed. It happens. When it does, there should be a person that can bring the group back in line with the guidelines everyone decided on and committed to.

Basically, whether you are a planner or a person who likes to wing it, when you bring other people together for a specific purpose in a professional manner, it is helpful for everyone to have an idea of what to expect and what is expected of them.

Spend some time creating some effective guidelines. Have everyone commit to following them. They can be changed or tweaked but starting out with a plan will help you be able to operate with fewer questions and less stress once you get up and running.

Once you have obtained agreement from each member about the general guidelines, you can begin to settle on the specifics for how your group will run.

> Get everyone's agreement and clear understanding on your general guidelines before moving on to a discussion about specific guidelines.

Chapter 6

Specific Guidelines for Critique Groups

After you have settled on the general guidelines for the purpose and character of your critique group and have gotten agreement by all members to abide by those guidelines, you can begin determining the specific guidelines for how you will run your group on an ongoing basis.

Some of these suggestions may seem trivial. The more things you can settle on up front, however, the smoother your group will run. So at least think through these issues so they will not sneak up on you unexpectedly.

Schedule

Whether you have an in-person or online critique group, it is important to have a submission schedule. You may settle on allowing each member to submit a piece for critique each time you meet or each week or month if online. But there should be an additional deadline for that submission. If the group schedule allows for David to submit the second week of the month, he should submit the Sunday or Monday of that week; not Saturday.

People need time to respond before the next week when new submissions will be received.

Having a submission schedule and a deadline date for submission, helps avoid blockages where people have too many pieces that need feedback in a short amount of time.

Set up a schedule and hold people to it.

On that same point, determine in advance how often members can *not* submit. Although we treasure feedback from other members, occasionally, our writing is not at a point where we want feedback. It is understandable therefore to not submit each time it is our turn.

Part of being a valuable member of a group however, is not just providing feedback to others but also of submitting our own work and the vulnerability and gratitude that goes with it. Additionally, having a sense about the style and content of a member's writing helps other members understand that person's feedback when critiquing other member's work.

Therefore, consider a rule that members are required to submit a piece for critique every second or third time, at a minimum.

Critiquing Deadline

Similarly, have a deadline for when critiques are due. Yes, life gets busy, but people are often waiting for feedback before making revisions or proceeding further on the project.

If your group's submission schedule is to submit a piece on Sunday or Monday, then a reasonable deadline for feedback would be by Saturday of that same week. You might decide to allow more time. But whatever you decide as a group, try to keep those deadlines consistent. If you are involved in the publishing industry, you will find that deadlines are one of the major things writers need to address. Adhering to deadlines within your group is great practice. And it is the thoughtful thing to do.

Follow-up Discussions

One of the most valuable parts of being in a critique group is often the follow-up discussions. For example, one member might simply indicate that the writer changed point of view. If three other people don't understand point of view, then shared information can help everyone learn—even the person who made the comment will learn through the exercise of explaining it.

Similarly, if one person suggests that a sub-plot might be needed at a certain point of a novel, a lively discussion of brainstorming possible plots or character troubles can help other people with problem areas in their own novels.

Revisions

Based on critiques and follow-up discussions, most writers find they will revise their work. They will naturally then want to know if the revision improved the piece. Did it resolve the issue? Make something clearer? Increase the value of the project?

Determine in advance then how you will handle re-submissions or revisions of the same work. If your group is small, and the piece is short, some groups will allow a revision to be submitted during the same time frame. For example, If Joanne submitted a piece on Sunday; received feedback on Monday and immediately implemented those suggestions. The group might allow her to resubmit that same revised piece that same week.

Or the group might require that Joanne wait for her next regularly scheduled time to submit the revision.

Size of Submission

Most groups will limit a submission to a certain number of words. Much of the determination will have to do with the number of members and turn-around time for feedback. A standard submission might be 2500 or 5000 words. Other groups might allow a single chapter.

Some groups prefer to allow a submission of an entire book at once, perhaps allowing each member to submit only one book per year. In that case, of course you would need to allow members a month or more for feedback and probably not have more than one person submit within that same time frame.

Decide what your guideline will be. Certainly, the group can make exceptions. But if everyone knows what to expect there will be fewer problems. Many groups might have a word limit of, say 2500 words. A person might submit a whole chapter of more than 2500 words with an indication of where the 2500 words ends. Readers have access to the rest of the chapter if they decide to continue reading but would not be required or expected to do so.

Submission Mechanics

Readers should not have to struggle with reading a submission. The publishing industry has specific guidelines for submissions received from writers. As a writer, we should become familiar with following submission guidelines.

It is reasonable therefore to have submission guidelines within a critique group also.

Here is an example of what you might have as mechanics for submission:

- A single piece of writing
- 1000-2500 words
- Sent via an e-mail attachment by midnight on the Monday before a scheduled meeting
- Format: Microsoft Word doc
- Double-spaced
- 12-point, New Times Romans font

Submission Requests

When you submit a piece of writing to the group it is helpful to tell the other members its genre and the market for it, if you have one in mind (a specific magazine, for example). Note any specific feedback you are looking for: plot, voice, logic, sequence, etc. or if you are looking for a general critique. Similarly, if you believe this is a final, final version, are you looking for tight copy editing on spelling, grammar and punctuation?

If members know how to be most helpful, it will be easier for them to focus on what you need.

Style Guide

Some people are especially passionate about commas or other aspects of grammar or punctuation. Lively discussions can ensue and can be a great learning experience for the group.

It can be helpful however, if your group settles on a single style guide (MLA, AP, Chicago, for example) and uses that when looking at all manuscripts. Of course, certain publishing houses and magazines require writers to follow specific style guides. If your group decides not to settle on a single style guide, then each member should specify during the submission whether she has used a specific style guide in the piece.

Feedback Mechanics

Similarly, determine how group members will provide feedback. First, it is important to provide a copy of the submission to each member well in advance of the meeting (if in person) or by the deadline (if online).

If it is for an in-person group, will members print out a hard copy of the piece at home, make hand-written notes on the paper and then read from the notes in person before giving the packet to the writer?

If it is for an online group, will members be required to use Microsoft Track Changes? If so, will each member be assigned a specific color to use for all submissions? Will each member add on to every other person's comments within that one document?

Or will members type changes into the original document using strike-overs and colored font for changes or comments?

Or will members simply type up a summary critique specifying general thoughts about the piece beginning at the start of the document through to the end?

Or will each member determine how they want to provide feedback themselves?

Whatever format the group or individual members determine for providing feedback, all feedback should be shared with every member of the group. For example, if the group is in person, the critique should be given aloud to the group. If the group is online, every member should receive a copy of every critique.

It is by sharing ideas and knowledge that all of us grow into stronger, more creative and more effective writers.

Specific guidelines will help the group run more smoothly. It can help to have one person facilitate the group at least for the first several months, just to remind members of the guidelines until they become familiar.

Chapter 7

Giving Critiques

If you're like me, you spend a minimum of an hour thinking about a critique and trying to give helpful feedback. And you have tried to do so with kindness, gentleness and respect.

Remember the "sandwich" formula for critiquing. Begin and end with a reassurance to the writer of what was good or admirable about the writing. Assuring the other writer that you see good in the writing helps the writer be more open to suggestions, because she will be more likely to recognize that your critique was given in order to be helpful and encouraging.

Sometimes, however your critique is totally ignored. It's not argued about; it is just passed over and the next time you receive the same manuscript (revised) none of your suggestions have been implemented. What do you do then?

One time a colleague asked me for feedback on a picture book. I made some suggestions about sequence and sent them off. I received the "revised" manuscript back within the hour asking, "is this better?" None of my suggestions had been addressed. I scratched my head, made the same comments and returned it.

The manuscript came back later that day with none of my suggestions implemented (again). I responded that I could offer no further help.

When the story came back to me again that day, I realized she had been sending it to several people. She would receive feedback from one person, implement some of it and then send it off again to everyone.

When it came back once more about a week later, some of my suggestions were implemented. The point here is that we don't always know what's going on at the other end of the critiques. It can be frustrating to give the same advice again and again and not have it even responded to.

So what else might be going on?

1) Remember that the piece you are critiquing is their story; not yours. We may have fabulous ideas, but our vision isn't always their vision. They must write *their* story; not ours. And we must let them.

2) Consider the possibility that your suggestion may not be clear to them. Yes, we're writers, but we all still struggle with clear communication. Perhaps you need to restate your idea or give an example of what you mean.

For example, a suggestion to "show don't tell" is standard writing advice. However, better might be an example. If a submission says the main character "danced across the room," we might infer that she is happy. However, if she waltzed across the room, we might gain information about her character, that perhaps she is a romantic, is in love or wants to be. Or if she twirls across the room like a ballerina, perhaps she values grace and beauty in the classical sense. If her dance is somewhere between hip hop and tribal, one of her character traits might be a sense of adventure or non-conformity.

3) Consider the possibility that you might be wrong. In the case of grammar and spelling, it is possible that you learned the rule incorrectly or have applied a technique improperly. I used to continually correct manuscripts in which the author had a character exclaim "What!" I had learned that "what" is a question. So, I would regularly critique that little word and turn the exclamation point into a question mark.

   I occasionally notice an exclamation point used after the word *what* in published work. Therefore, it is no longer one of my hot buttons. The point (!) is I had to concede that the critique comment I was pushing (aside from not being the biggest issue in a writer's toolbox) might have come from my misunderstanding of a grammar rule.

Remember that a writer is not required to agree with every comment received. Nor is a writer required to implement even one suggestion received.

If, however, you find that most of your suggestions to all of the members of your critique group are ignored, consider the possibility that the problem is your side and not theirs. In that case, seek to find out what you may not understand correctly—either a rule or your reading of other people's work.

In addition, consider reviewing whatever background information the person provided for the piece. What feedback are they specifically looking for? What type of help do they need? If they are looking for structural thoughts, then pointing out the use of a comma is of marginal value.

On the other hand, if the manuscript is in the final stage of completion when they are looking for a copy edit, and you suggest a total restructuring of the book, including renaming characters and placing the entire story on Mars, then your stellar (pun intended) critique suggestions are equally of marginal value.

Remember that this is their book; not yours. You are free to write your own story set on Mars and place commas wherever you see fit, as long as you claim your grammar is based on the Martian language, not the *Oxford Guide to English Grammar*.

Now you have some thoughts on how to *give* feedback. *Receiving* feedback is just the opposite, right?

Not entirely.

> When giving critiques, remember that the goal is to make the other person's writing clearer; *not* to turn their writing into your vision.

Chapter 8

Receiving Critiques

Just like there is a way to give critiques with kindness, grace and respect, there is also a way to receive them. Here are a few tips:

Think about every comment

At first glance, a comment may feel completely wrong. You shake your head and wonder where in the world that idea came from. Your tendency is to dismiss it instantly. But if you have been working with your critique group (or even if you are all new to each other) recognize that every member takes writing seriously.

Assume that they, like you, spend considerable time and thought in providing a critique. Take their thought seriously and look for something that might have caused their comment. They may have sensed an issue early in the piece that needed to be addressed, but have commented on something later in the manuscript, at a point where the comment doesn't seem to fit. Look therefore, at the comment in terms of the whole manuscript; rather than thinking it refers to a single sentence. In other words, sometimes a person senses there is an issue but can't exactly explain why, so they make a general statement later, hoping you will know what they mean.

For example, if you have stated that the theme of your novel is learning to trust but the main character keeps hopping into cars with strangers, then the critique member might feel that such actions are an issue to address. In your mind, however, the theme of "learning to trust" might be less about physical safety and more about the heart. In other words, perhaps you have not made your theme as clear as it needs to be. So, take each comment seriously and consider it before tossing it aside.

It is OK to ask for clarification

Maybe you need to ask why the person had that comment. As long as you ask the question without sounding defensive, you can often have great group discussions about the craft of writing and can brainstorm ways to work around issues.

Remember that your story or non-fiction point is clear in your head. The struggle is presenting it so it is clear to others.

If you agree with the comment made, make the change, especially if more than one person makes the same comment. If you don't initially agree, spend some time in thought. Let the idea sit for a bit. Think how it might change the rest of your project—either to confuse things or clarify them or take them into a new direction. Then if you agree, do it.

If you don't agree with the comment, don't make the change. Even if you greatly admire the person who made the suggestion and know they're knowledgeable about the craft of writing, you don't have to make the change they suggest. It is possible the person doesn't understand the genre you are writing or the market for whom you are writing. In fact, even fabulous suggestions might be completely inappropriate for your particular project.

Real rules vs. personal taste

Recognize that some comments may be about real issues, real writing rules or real questions to be addressed. Other comments may be about personal taste—not only preference in genre but also about things such as writing in first person or third person omniscient.

I love writing and reading in first person, but some people only like third person past. Some people like present tense. That drives me crazy to read, but I recognize that these are personal preferences and any comments about things of personal preference are not necessarily helpful. They are still things to consider however—if not for this project; then for something I might write in the future.

It may require hard work

Consider the possibility that you don't like a comment because changing it would be scary or difficult. If something in a comment makes you hesitate, despite your initial "no!" reaction, give it some time. There may be some truth to the suggestion and you just need to get over yourself and work at making the project the best it can be.

Fix for clarity

If the comment is a matter of clarity, fix the issue. Maybe it is completely clear to you. Remember however, that as writers it is our job to write with clarity. If someone doesn't understand what we have written, then it is our job to change how it is written so it is clearly understood.

Each reader comes to a piece with a unique background and perspective. Although we try to write for a broad readership, we must still strive for clarity. Assume your critique partner is intelligent with a desire to help you make your writing as clear as possible.

Check for yourself

If the comment has to do with spelling, grammar or punctuation and you are not sure about the actual rule, look it up. Remember that styles in publishing—even when it comes to grammar and punctuation—change over time.

I grew up learning that you were required to have a comma following items in a series, including a comma immediately before the *and* (this comma is known as the *Oxford comma*). When I got my first book contract, my editor (for a respected educational publisher) took out each and every one of those commas. It was hard to change my thinking of 40 years of comma placement, but I learned that the rule in publication had changed (at least for that publisher). So, I changed too. It was a matter of a particular *style guide.* If you don't know what a *style guide* in the publishing industry is, you need to research and find out. (See Chapter 6)

Remember though that in fiction (and to a lesser extent in non-fiction also) sometimes grammar and punctuation rules can be broken for effect.

Like here.

Notice the words *Like here* above is not a proper sentence. But I used them for effect to make the exception stand out. In other words, understand the rules and know when it is appropriate to break them.

If a critique group member points out that you have broken the rule, you can then change it or leave it for the effect you intended.

It's not personal

Try not to take suggestions personally. Remember that the other members of your critique group are there to help you make your project better. They are not there to tear your baby apart or tear you down.

Sometimes no matter how hard we try to give feedback with kindness, grace and respect, the feedback just smarts. But try to be objective and look, not at how you feel about the way a comment sounds, but instead at what it says—whether it is possible that the comment, taken objectively might indeed make the writing better.

Now you're part of an active, supportive critique group. You've got all the feedback you need, right? Maybe.

Or maybe not.

> Critiques can sometimes smart. When we remember that the other person is trying to be helpful and encouraging, it can help us see comments and suggestions clearly and appreciate them more.

Chapter 9

Writing Partners and Beta Readers

In addition to critique groups, writing partners and beta readers are wonderful resources to make our writing better. These are something between having a super tiny critique group and your own personal editor.

Rather than or in addition to submitting your work to a group of other writers, you might settle on one or two writers you trust and admire. You would meet online or in person periodically to discuss your projects, brainstorm and get help throughout the project. A writing partner is a helper in your writing. You are not both working on the same project. Rather, you are partnering to help with each other's individual writing projects.

A writing partner is part critique group; part developmental editor. A writing partner is someone who walks with you during the entire process of a project. And you with her.

A beta reader on the other hand, generally comes in at the end of a project—after your final revision and before publication. The beta reader reads the project and looks at it as a whole—sequence, tone, voice, vocabulary, chapter topics and organization for non-fiction projects and voice, plot, subplots, character development, pacing, setting and other fiction writing elements for fiction projects. The beta reader is also on the lookout for copy edits—grammar, spelling, clarity.

A beta reader is part critique group and part copy editor. She comes along side at the end of your project but before it heads out into the world.

So, which do you need? Or do you need both?

I love having a critique group. I love getting feedback on my project from multiple people as I am in the process of writing. I find that comments one person may say lead me into 14 different directions I'd not considered before. I also find that when I give feedback on multiple people's projects, I learn more about my craft. Sometimes I find that a comment I have made to three other members is actually something I need to address in my own writing.

I also love having a writing partner who believes in me and my writing and I in her. A one-on-one relationship results in and develops trust. As you work together, you understand each other's style and purpose at a deeper level. That enables more effective feedback and suggestions as well as more enthusiastic encouragement.

I also love having a few beta readers look at my finished project. Those trusted and valued colleagues know what I'm trying to accomplish and value my writing enough to make sure I reach the level of writing I want to reach. I also find that a fabulous beta reader does not necessarily need to be an accomplished writer.

It is helpful if a beta reader has a grasp of grammar, punctuation and spelling, but at this point, I am more interested in the general: does what I say make sense? Does it flow? Am I missing anything that should be included? Or have I included too much and resulted in something cumbersome?

If my beta reader loves books; especially if he loves reading in my genre, then what he has to say about my book will be extremely valuable, whether it comes from the point of view of a writer or a reader. If he is not a writer, he may not know that I have switched mid book from active voice to passive voice, but as a reader, he will know that it doesn't flow properly at that point.

If I have submitted my manuscript to my critique group or if I have worked with a writing partner, most of those "craft of writing" issues will have been resolved by now. The beauty of a beta reader is that I now can receive feedback from the point of view of a reader—which is who I am writing for in the first and last place.

So, writer friend, is an in-person critique group what you need? Or an online group? Or one or two writing partners? Or a few beta readers at the end of your project?

Or all of the above?

What feels right to you? Are you ready to get started writing in community with others?

> Whether you are in a critique group, have a writing partner and/or beta reader, feedback from other people who care about your writing is invaluable.

Part Two:

Group Horn Tooting

Chapter 10

Joint Marketing

Hopefully, you are now thinking about how you—as a member of a writing community—can work with other writers; how you can benefit and grow your craft and how you can help other writers grow their craft, too.

Now, let's add something to the mix.

As authors, we don't just write books. We also have to get those books into the hands of readers. That means marketing.

Branding/platform building is about figuring out what you represent. For my step-by-step thoughts on branding, see my book in the Writer's Book Shelf Series *The Write Brand: Becoming Known in the World.* (Shameless self-promotion? Nope. I believe in the value of that book to writers. Read on for exactly why I include that statement here.)

Marketing is about promoting a specific product.

There are tons of books on marketing in general. There are even a few hundred thousand books about book marketing. Before you embark on a successful marketing plan for your book, however, you first you must fully believe and endorse an enormous truth:

Marketing is about serving others.

You must believe in your books. If you don't believe that your books are of value, then why would you offer them for sale to others? Why would you even bother writing them? So first, believe that there is value in your writing. My mantra is "even if only one person benefits from what I write, that is enough."

Market your work with that one person in mind. Focus on how what you have created can benefit him. Maybe it is a life lesson and years of pain you will save him from through your work. Maybe it is a chuckle from a single line in a book you have written that brightens your reader's day. Whatever the takeaway is from your writing, focus on that. Make it big. Make it important in your own mind. Focus on that so you can get over yourself. Get over the image of you hunched over, face to the ground, holding your book out in trembling hands, hoping someone will take pity on you and buy your book.

What you have created is of value. Repeat that statement out loud.

What I have created is of value.

When you offer something of value to someone who will benefit from it, you are serving them. Do so with a generous, honest and cheerful heart. Your book may not be of value to every person in the world. Focus your attention, your thoughts and your heart on the ones who will care.

The key to marketing is in the value we bring. If our books have no value, then strutting our stuff and marketing our books is prideful. But if what we have written has the possibility of helping even one person, then we have the responsibility to do what we can to help that one person find our book.

Now you know why I placed that "shameless self-plug" for my branding book in this chapter. I believe in that book and the value it offers to writers. Please, reader—do the same. Your book is of value to someone. Focus on that person and offer your book as a way of serving them.

Once you understand that marketing is about offering something of value to others, you can take a second step in marketing.

Follow the Golden Rule of marketing: Do unto other writers as you would have them do unto you.

Early in my publishing career I whined to someone that I hated marketing. It felt wrong, I said, to spend time tooting my own horn. "Why?" they asked me.

I thought about it a bit and then replied, "I feel like I'm playing a kazoo and I want to play a French horn. When I listen to the marketing music I make, I don't like the sound. And I don't like the attention."

That realization began a thought process that has become an important part of the "business side" of my writing career.

If I wanted my kazoo to sound better, not only did I need to practice more, I needed to study kazoo playing. I also needed to play with other kazoo players until maybe all of us could sound less like kazoo players and more like the symphony orchestra we imagined in our heads. Or a rock band.

The idea of joint marketing was formed.

What do I mean?

If I feel uncomfortable or insecure marketing my book, can I market someone else's book for them and can they in turn market mine? I don't mean hiring each other as a personal publicist. But if I can enthusiastically include my colleague's book in my pitch about my book in the same genre, doesn't that make the pitch stronger? If nothing else, it subtly reinforces the underlying truth that the topic is important. Therefore, maybe the person I am pitching to will more easily see that something I have to say in my book is also important.

Every time I do so, and every time I receive feedback from my colleague when she pitches my book, won't I gain confidence and have more encouragement to toot my own horn a bit louder in harmony with hers?

If you responded earlier, that yes, as a writer, you want to serve your readers by offering them the value of your books, and that yes, you want to help other writers do the same, what does that mean in terms of marketing?

Read on.

> How might looking at marketing as serving others (both your readers and other writers) help you get over part of the difficulty you face in marketing?

Chapter 11

Setting Up a Joint Marketing Group

Sometimes a critique group or group of writing partners will gradually add marketing to the things they do for and with each other.

Other times, members of a critique group have no interest in marketing. In that case, you may need to look beyond your critique group for other writers eager to work together on marketing.

First, just as you did when setting up or finding a critique group or writing partner, you need to gather together like-minded authors.

In the same way you find writers for critiquing, get involved in writer's clubs. Join a local book club. Be a regular customer at bookstores you would like to have your book in. Become familiar with people who work at and visit your local libraries. Attend local author events. Ask bookstores and libraries if they have any groups or events for aspiring authors.

Once you have found one or more authors to work with, be thinking about how you might market each other.

The simplest way you can help each other is to include that other person's book in a pitch about your book of the same genre, knowing they are doing the same for you.

Sharing both books in a pitch also subtly reinforces the overall importance of the topic. Maybe the reader you are talking with never *knew* that there was a specific fiction genre of polar bear mysteries (is there one?) But if you share two titles in that genre with a reader, maybe that fact alone will intrigue the reader to become a new fan of both your book and your colleague's. In other words, sharing a colleague's book, not only markets their work and yours, it also gives credibility to your work.

In addition, your mention of your colleague's book is perceived as valuable because you have no financial interest in that book. The person you are speaking with subtly understands that you are not all about the money; you are not all about pushing your own book. The person understands that you are serving them—the reader—sharing the value of both books and letting them take it from there.

What also happens, is that every time you pitch your book and your colleague's book together, you gain confidence in marketing. When you share the value of both books with others, it reinforces the value of your own book in your mind. You are continuously reminded that your book is of value. The more you are reminded, the more you believe. The more you believe, the easier marketing becomes: serving your reader by offering something of value.

Start small. If you are part of a critique group, no doubt eventually another member of your group will publish a book. Often writers will place a note in the front matter of the book, formally thanking the other members of their critique for helping get the book written and written well.

From your point of view, you may have spent a year or more working on that book with your colleague—making suggestions, helping with grammar or other aspects of the writing. You have spent hours of your own time helping turn that book into what it became.

You have a sense of ownership in that book.

Writers work together to make books better and to get them into the hands of readers. When we have a hand in a book's creation—even one without our name on the cover—we want to help readers find the book.

When other writers help us in our book's creation, they want to help readers find our book.

There is a community of writers. We love books. We love readers. We want to connect books and readers—especially our books, but also books we love and believe in even if they were written by someone else.

If you have helped someone create a book and they have helped you, the two of you are the perfect people to join together in getting your books into the hands of readers. You already have a sense of ownership; of duty; a love for that book. Share that love with others.

That's a simple example of how to jointly market books for each other. But there are other specific marketing activities you can do with other writers. It's not about taking out an ad in the *New York Times.*

Most of us couldn't afford that anyway.

Let's look then at some other marketing activities we can do with other writers.

Who do you know who might be interested in working with you to market each other's books? If you don't know anyone, how will you reach out to find writers?

Chapter 12

Reciprocal Book Reviews

Readers have a million choices when it comes to what book to read. Honest book reviews are often what sell a book to a reader even more than the book description.

I may have written the most awesome back cover copy that tells a reader that they should not only buy my book, they should buy 10 copies and give them to their friends.

While what my back copy says may be true, that marketing jargon is from me—someone with a financial interest in the book.

How much more impactful is it if someone who has no financial interest in my book says the same thing? That's the power of book reviews.

It is hard to get people to review your book, you say. Other writers are in the same boat. They too need book reviews. So why not, help each other? If I knew someone else would be posting an honest book review on my book, I am always that much happier to post one for them. Yes, it takes time to read the book and effort to create a review that is helpful and honest. But if you and another colleague have agreed to each review a book of the other person, the results are worth the time and effort: a review for your book and knowing you've encouraged and helped another writer.

That is what is meant by *reciprocal book reviews*. Two authors read and review each other's books.

What if you don't read that genre? That may not be relevant if you have first joined up with authors who write the genre you do. But what if you are asked to read a genre you hate?

Then you focus your review, not on the story but on something you do like. Maybe the main character has a fantastic voice. Or the bad guy is delightfully horrible. Or perhaps the theme comes across well or the world creation is especially unique. Focus on what you like or admire about the writing.

But make sure you can give the book a good review. It is not helpful for you to write a bad review. In fact, no review is better than a bad review. If you feel the book doesn't deserve a good review from you—don't lie. But offer something to the author instead. Here are a few ideas:

- Offer to review their next book. Or a different one.
- Offer to interview the author instead and post the interview on your website.
- Offer to let the author do a guest post on your blog and let them talk about the book.
- Offer an idea or two about where the author might market the book.

Overall, be encouraging.

Sometimes people (even writers) will tell us they loved our book. When we thank them and ask them to leave a review on Amazon (and yes, you should ask them!), they hem and haw, ultimately confessing that they've never done one and don't know how.

They are not talking about never having done a book review—after all, everyone did book reviews in grammar school. Rather, they are saying that they don't know what buttons to click to get their comments to post on the Amazon website.

Don't let that be an excuse for people who love your book not to leave a review.

At the end of this book—Appendix I—I have included a step-by-step guide to posting a review on Amazon. Copy this guide yourself. Or rewrite it to make it your own. Post the how-to on your website. Print it and hand it out when you sign copies of your book for your friends.

Or include the instructions at the end of your book, after the final chapter, right on the page where you say:

If you enjoyed this book, please consider leaving a review at Amazon.com. Here is how to do so.

Make it easy for people to love your book and share it with other readers who will love it too.

Although any book review that is honest and helpful is wonderful marketing, there are a few things to do and don't do when posting a review.

- Do *not* say your daughter (mother/brother/grandson/best friend) wrote this book. People are looking for information on why the book is good; not why the author is loved.

- Don't argue with other reviews. Those readers are entitled to an opinion. Starting an argument brings focus on the bad review.

- If you don't want to review the book's specific content, can you review one aspect of the book? Perhaps you appreciated the writing, the author's approachable tone, the story line, one of the characters, the setting or theme. Every good review helps an author find an audience.

If you have a book for sale on Amazon, encourage your readers to post reviews. If you don't yet have a book for sale on Amazon, post reviews for other writers' books. Sometimes practicing aspects of marketing by helping market other people's books will make you more comfortable when it's time to market your own work.

Plus, reciprocity and cross-promotion are one of the best and easiest way to get started in marketing and keep going for the long haul. If you are out helping other writers promote their books, they are more willing to write helpful reviews for your baby when it steps out into the world. With so many books to choose from, honest reviews are a service to others.

Remember also that those Amazon reviews are public. In other words, once they are posted, you can use them for your own purpose.

- If you redo your book or front cover, quote one or two reviews on the back cover. Use only the first name or initials unless it's someone famous or well-known.

- Use the quotes on your webpage where your book cover is displayed.

- Use the quotes anywhere and everywhere—at in-person book sales events; fliers; other promotion.

Book reviews are one of the most powerful ways you can encourage prospective readers to buy your book. Because all authors know the value of positive book reviews, they are usually more than willing to work with other authors on reciprocal book reviews.

Reciprocal book reviews can be a rewarding and simple way for authors to help market each other.

Who might be willing to reciprocate with you to do a book review for each other?

Chapter 13

Cooperative Blogging

We all know we should have an online presence. The most widely accepted marketing advice for developing an online presence is regular, consistent blogging. Blogging gets your name in front of readers on a reoccurring basis. It also provides a way for you to create a platform for other writing activities and projects.

Blogging can also be a powerful marketing tool because it is a venue where you can remind your readers of the value of your book. If you have written a book about growing a vegetable garden in your kitchen window, having a weekly blog with gardening tips, nutritional information or recipes can be a continuous reminder that—by-the-way—you might want to check out my book, too.

Blogging can also be a powerful *joint* marketing tool as you and your joint marketing colleagues promote each other's books and share your readership. Let's look at some ways to pursue cooperative blogging.

Guest Posting

If you and another colleague (or several) decide to pursue this type of marketing, you might each guest post on each other's blog sites. You might do this one time, from time to time, or on a scheduled, reoccurring basis.

Even if your colleague has no book in print at the time, you can offer them a place to practice their craft and to explore the world of being published. And if they have a blog site while they are building a platform in preparation for their book release, their readers may also become your readers.

In a similar way, many blog sites have an open invitation to other writers to post from time to time on their site. Look into those as opportunities to share reciprocal posting.

If a member of your joint marketing group does not have a website, they might be encouraged to set up a free blogsite to begin an online presence. Even a professional writing page on social media can provide an opportunity to post and thus reciprocally help market each other.

Create a posting network

Instead of just two people sharing posts, consider creating a network. Sometimes called a blogging network, blog hop or blog chain, this banding of several people can be effective in marketing each other and sharing readership.

For example, a group of four people might each write a guest post one time a month. That post would show up on the other three sites and theirs on their week of the month. You could select a word or theme for all members to write about or leave it open, based on your like-mindedness as authors.

The beauty of cooperative blogging is how readership is shared. For example, when I post on your website, I will leave a note on my website that I'm posting on your site that day. Then I provide a link for my readers to go over there and read what I have to say. Perhaps, some of my readers will poke around your website, like what they see and subscribe to your site.

At the same time, on your website, you will post my article, along with a link to my website. Perhaps, some of your readers will like my article and click on the link to my website, like what they see there and subscribe to my site.

The point of cooperative blogging is to share readership.

***My Example*:** For several years I was part of a blog chain of 10 people. Each month we selected a theme. Every member of the chain wrote one post on that theme and signed up for a date that month to post.

Every member then uploaded onto their own site a schedule of dates for posting during the month with the link to all of our sites. When the blog posted that day, each member announced the post on whatever social media we were part of. Our individual readers were encouraged to read what all writers had to say about that theme each month.

Even if you are not part of a cooperative blogging group, try helping other writers by offering them a place to post. You will gain benefits for yourself.

My Example: During the time I was writing solely for the children's educational market, I invited other children's authors to guest post on my site. They provided a short activity kids could do that taught something based on their children's book. They linked to my site. I then put their activity up, book cover and link onto a separate page on my website called "Books that Teach."

Obviously, this benefited the other writers by increased visibility, having a location for their books to be highlighted, publicity for their book and a direct link for my readers to purchase their book.

It also benefited me:

- It made my website richer while other authors provided the content
- It helped promote my brand to parents, kids and teachers as an author in educational market
- My site became known as a resource for parents and teachers
- It gave me a reputation in the writing community as an encourager
- It elevated my educational books by being part of a larger children's literature community
- I learned techniques of marketing I could implement on my own projects
- Many of those colleagues reciprocated by plugging my books
- I made friends

One of the beautiful things about helping other writers is that sometimes you are benefited, even if no one is reciprocating.

So, look for other writers to share blogging with—one on one or as part of a group, one time or on an ongoing basis. But if you can't find a person or group to work with, you might still find rewards in just helping others.

Do you have a blog? Who do you know who might cooperate with you?

Chapter 14

Joint Newsletters and Fliers

A hot button in marketing for the last few years has been the importance sending out digital newsletters. Whether you have 20 subscribers or 20,000, there is truth to the advice that a newsletter can be a lovely marketing tool.

But having a newsletter must make sense for you.

I've been blogging at least once a week for over ten years. I figure that any "news" I have to tell my readers can probably wait until Monday. Therefore, I haven't had a driving desire to create a newsletter. But I recognize that a newsletter is a good idea and in fact receive several lovely newsletters from other writing colleagues.

You may not be at a point in your writing career where you have enough news or valuable information to share with your readers on a monthly or even quarterly basis.

A great alternative might be a joint newsletter. A joint newsletter would bring together three or four authors. Each would provide content for each newsletter; making the newsletter entertaining and informative. This becomes a fabulous place for book release announcements for colleagues.

The other great thing about a joint newsletter is that if 4 people band together and each author only has 500 subscribers; that means together they have 2000 people they can reach jointly. Once again, this idea of a joint newsletter is about sharing readership.

***My Newsletter Example*:** Although I was not ready to have a newsletter myself, several years ago I recognized the potential marketing power of doing so. I therefore wanted to learn the software involved in creating and sending out a digital newsletter, so I would be prepared to put my own newsletter out one day. A paid membership writing group I belonged to wanted to launch a monthly newsletter to go out to over 1,000 subscribers. I jumped at the opportunity and volunteered to edit and publish the digital newsletter for a year.

Although this is not an example of a joint newsletter, it is another example of how my helping other writers benefited me:

- I learned a new software technology and my brain didn't explode in the process.

- Promoting other members through interviews, release announcements and guest posts gave me more experience doing marketing activities.

- I created and wrote a monthly "column" in that newsletter about the craft of writing, which helped me become known in our writing community as a professional writer.

- As editor and writer of that column, I had a byline which meant my name and book titles were in front of over 1,000 readers each month—along with an electronic link to my website.

For those writers who remain terrified of technology (despite my assurance that if I can do it without boxes of Kleenex to sop up the tears, you can, too), there is another low-tech alternative: a printed flier.

In this case, you might either create a trifold, semi-permanent flier with information on your group of joint marketing members. Or you might create a single page flier and hand deliver or mail it using the US Postal Service. You definitely get more "bang for your buck" digitally, but still, a flier is a viable alternative.

***My Flier Example*:** I was part of an online children's book group with members who lived in three countries. Some members were published; some were not, but all of us were committed to writing for children.

We created a trifold pamphlet. Each member was highlighted with a photo and short bio, a website link if they had one and a description of what they wrote. Each person then printed off pamphlets at home and took them to all events involving books and/or writing. We passed them out wherever we went, thus marketing all members of our group across the United States, Canada and Europe.

At a Society of Children's Book Writers & Illustrators conference, I handed the pamphlet to a wearied acquisitions editor for a major New York children's publisher. She took the pamphlet politely, then her demeanor changed. She straightened up, looked at me and said enthusiastically, "This is a fabulous idea!"

Editors—especially the editors who offer writers book contracts—understand the importance of writers becoming known and creating a platform. They also appreciate whatever marketing experience and plans authors have to promote their books. If an acquisitions editor thought a printed pamphlet to market several children's authors was a fabulous idea, you can be sure it is—no matter how low tech.

Certainly, you can reach more people for less money by sending out a digital newsletter. But a flier can be effective, especially if you and your colleagues do in-person events. It can also get you started until that day when all of you in your group have exciting publishing news to share.

In which case, you might decide to go for the digital newsletter, after all.

Who might you join up with to do a newsletter? Or would a low-tech flier be something you and others could pass out at in-person events?

Chapter 15

Interviews

For several years I posted an interview of an author colleague on my blog each month. I created several sets of general interview questions which I forwarded to the author. I then posted the interview along with the author's photo and bio, book cover and link to purchase. The author I interviewed then posted a link on her website to my interview, sending her readers over to my site.

This idea is similar to the idea in Chapter 12 of cooperative blogging where you send each other's readers to each other's sites, in the hope that both of your readerships will grow.

Interviews however can be a great way to switch things up. They are fun for readers; can be visually appealing on the screen and can enrich your website as well as your search engine optimization (SEO) as you provide links to the interviewee's site as well as a link to their book.

The easiest way to get started is to first interview writers you know; doing reciprocal interviews of each other. This will likely be a one-time event although you could also interview each other whenever one of you releases a new book.

When you feel comfortable doing interviews in general, you can then approach other authors—even well-established ones.

Remember that all authors appreciate help and the opportunity to become known in your little world. Approach authors and become known as an encourager. Even if they don't reciprocate, you might be able to bring a few of their fans to your site.

One critique group I was a member of interviewed each other, posting one interview each week on each other's sites over several months.

But I have also interviewed writers separately even though they did not reciprocate. Here's what I did:

I contacted members of an online writing forum I was part of. I forwarded general interview questions to each author who then emailed me her answers. I posted the interview on my website, along with her photo and bio, book cover and link to purchase. The author I interviewed then posted a link on her website to my interview, sending her readers over to my site.

I did this monthly for several years with different authors. The benefits to me were:

- I had material for posting to my website that required little work on my part.
- I became known as an encourager to other writers, many of whom showed me gratitude by plugging my books.
- My interviews were helpful to my readers who were interested in the genre the other authors wrote.
- I felt a deeper connection with the writing community as I began to approach people outside of my own network and found that established and well-known authors were struggling with marketing just like I was.

If you decide to interview authors, first approach those within your personal writing network. Even if some writers are not yet published, an interview gives them a chance to talk about their work in progress and helps them build up a readership for when their book is released.

As I did, you might start doing interviews by developing a set of questions to give to each interviewee. You might vary some of the questions, depending on the genre of the author and have an open-ended final question, giving the interviewee an opportunity to express anything you haven't asked.

Once you feel comfortable interviewing authors, you might then create unique questions for each author. Or you might continue with the same interview set, which provides continuity for your readers who might use your interviews to sort through information to become new fans of your interviewee.

Appendix II at the end of this book, contains two sets of general interview questions I have used in the past. Interviews need not be deeply probing or filled with revelation. The idea is to introduce your readers to other authors and share the fan base between writers.

When you feel comfortable doing interviews, approach other authors—even highly successful ones.

***My Example*:** I once read a book I enjoyed. So, I posted a review on Amazon. I then found the author's website and left a comment that I had reviewed the book. She responded, and we chatted about writing. I then asked her if she'd do an interview for my site and she excitedly agreed. She later read and reviewed one of my books in return.

Every author, no matter how many books they've written or how successful they are, appreciates marketing help.

Do you know an author you might interview on your website, blog site or social media?

Chapter 16

Speaker's Group

Words are the tools we writers use to get our message into the world. One way we build a platform or fan base is by stepping into a room where we can share our message personally. It can be hard to approach groups about speaking engagements. Or we might not have any idea what we could even speak about.

Creating a speaker's group and having each member of the group brainstorm engagements, topics of talks and ways to market each other as a speaker makes it easier.

A speaker's group is also a way for members to practice talks live. Using Skype, Facetime or meeting in person allows members to give each other feedback on tone, eye contact, gestures, things that might be missing from the talk or might be added.

You can also help each other create talks. Or you can create a talk or workshop you all present together.

Public speaking can be enormously rewarding. You get to meet the people you write for and who will be buying and reading your books. You may even find the prospect lucrative, from speaking fees as well as book sales at the event.

My Example: For children's writers, the number one marketing advice is to do school visits. A few years ago, I called out to members of the Society of Children's Book Writers and Illustrators living in my geographical area. I asked who was interested in creating a speaker's bureau for school visits. I received a response from 11 published authors that first day. Here is what we did:

- We met for lunch, so we were more than a name online.
- We brought our books, so we could be familiar with each other's work.
- We each reviewed one book for each member on Amazon. If nothing else, each of us had at least 11 positive book reviews for our books.
- We each agreed that we would be willing to travel anywhere within the geographical region represented by the members to speak at schools.
- We each created a bio and 2-sentence summary of a talk we might give to a school.
- I created a flier with the bios and talk summaries and emailed it to each member to print out.
- We each hand delivered and/or mailed a personal letter and flier to every school in our individual community.

As a group of twelve people, we were able to cover nearly 100 miles of geographical area and approached over a hundred schools for the group.

Additionally, by creating our own speaker's bureau, we instantly gained credibility as professional writers and speakers.

Public speaking is often referred to as one of the most terrifying things a person can face. But it doesn't have to be. The more you do it, the easier it becomes—especially when you are speaking with the people who you are writing for. Meeting those people gives a face to that reader you sit down at the computer and type out books for.

A speaker's group can help you get over your fear, find your voice, develop your topic and schedule events—all as you are doing the same for others.

Have you ever considered speaking to groups about your book or other topic related to your writing? How might a speaker's group encourage you or give you confidence to do so?

Chapter 17

Publish an Anthology

An anthology is a book collection of shorter works. Usually anthologies are based around a common theme or purpose. The theme might be faith or motivation or parenthood. A common purpose might be a gathering of local authors who write stories and longer articles about the history, geography or people in that community.

An example of an anthology most people have heard of is the *Chicken Soup* anthologies. Each year the publisher of the *Chicken Soup* anthologies lists upcoming themes that will be published. There is then a call out for submissions by authors to write on that theme.

The beauty of an anthology is that each contributor to the anthology shares their readers. For example, if I have an article in an anthology, my mother will definitely buy a copy of the book because she loves everything I do. And she will tell all her friends to buy a copy of the book, or she will buy them a copy as a gift.

When she reads my article, she will also read the stories written by the other contributors and might decide to read more of what they have written. So will my mother's friends. And the other writers' mothers and friends.

An anthology is an example of how a book can be used as an effective marketing tool for your other books.

One of the benefits of writing in this age of independent publishing, is that we can create our own anthologies. Here is how you might do this:

Gather together 10 or 20 writers and agree on a theme or purpose for the anthology (and a title). Each writer should write two or three stories so that the finished book is of adequate size. Or, after the original group has provided their stories, your group might open up submissions to other writers, in exchange for receiving a copy or two of the finished book.

- The group would critique and proof each other's work to assure a quality product.
- One person would oversee cover creation.
- One person would monitor styles and book formatting.
- One person would be responsible for uploading the final cover and manuscript onto the appropriate publishing platform.
- One person would oversee royalty distribution.
- Everyone would be responsible for marketing the book individually and together when possible.

Obviously, creating an anthology is a time-consuming project. But it can also be a great way to showpiece each other's work and share readership because as we promote our own stories in the anthology, we are also promoting every other writer in the book.

An anthology is also a fabulous way to get a publishing credit. Especially if you are pursuing traditional publishing, being part of a published anthology can help show your professionalism as a published author. It is also a great experience to learn manuscript formatting issues that are art of the publication process.

My Example: I have been part of three anthologies put out by Inspire Christian Writers. While an Inspire member, I also led two genre-specific critique groups. Leading those critique groups gave me "nagging rights" to encourage the group members to participate in the anthologies, making sure the stories went through the critique/revision process so that they were accepted easily for inclusion into the anthology.

Whether you decide to create an anthology as part of a joint marketing activity or submit to an existing anthology, it can be a great opportunity for joint marketing.

Who do you know who might be interested in creating an anthology?

Chapter 18

Create a Joint Website

Writers are regularly whacked over the head with the marketing advice that we *must have an online presence*. It is great advice.

Many writers however, tremble when facing the technology learning curve and don't even know how to start. Other writers don't have the couple hundred dollars each year to maintain a website or are overwhelmed with the work involved in providing continuously new and fresh content.

Even blogsites, most of which are free, have many of the same concerns for writers—the technology, the lack of direction, the work commitment.

Consider then a joint website.

Even if some or all of the writers in the group are still unpublished, having an online presence can help them become established online and build up a fan base and platform for when they become published.

Having an online presence also provides a place to send agents and editors when pursuing traditional publishing.

Remember the acquisitions editor I mentioned in chapter 13? Agents and editors want to know that an author is serious about writing and marketing. They don't ask for publishing credits and author bios just to get you to provide a writing sample. They want to see that you have a presence and a commitment to market your work. The publishing industry is a multi-million-dollar business. If they invest in you by buying your book, they want to be able to assure their acquisitions department that you will help your book be successful.

A simple way you might design a joint website would be:

- The website could have an active, changing home page. Each person could commit to writing a post once a week or once a month so that there is always new and fresh content.

- Create a separate web page for each person. There each person could write a bio, what they write and for whom and what books or other work they have published or are working on.

- You might have a separate web page to list all of the books written by all of the members. They could be listed alphabetically by title or listed by genre so that it is less obvious if one person has written 50 books and the rest have only written one. Of course, make sure each book title has a link to purchase that book either online or directly from the author.

- You might have an additional page of special posts or information or FAQs about the overall theme or purpose of the website. For example, if the website is dedicated to helping other writers, you might post individual articles about various writing tools or aspects of the craft of writing. If the purpose of your website is to encourage busy mothers, you might have a page dedicated to simple, healthy recipes kids love.

And, of course, each member would invite their own friends, family members and readers to visit and subscribe to the site.

My Example: Not every person in a critique group I was a member of had a published book. But we all knew the importance of platform building—back when that term had not yet been coined. At that time, websites were still coded using html, rather than drop and drag. But because one of our members was html savvy, she created a website for us. Each member instantly had an online location to showcase their work—either their published books or writing samples in the case of those members who were still unpublished. For the unpublished members, it was a location they could send agents and editors to show their professionalism and dedication to writing and marketing.

You may not think you are ready for your own website either because you are just beginning your writing career, don't yet have a book in print or can't afford the cost. Creating a joint website might be a wonderful option for you. Not only does it provide you with a low-cost online presence, the group can create a richer website more quickly with each member providing content at the start.

Whether or not you already have your own website, participating with other writers can increase your online presence.

Chapter 19

Create a Launch or Signing Group

You excitedly release a book and then wonder why the phone isn't ringing with offers to turn your novel into a blockbuster movie or hand you the Pulitzer for your brilliant non-fiction. Let's fact the fact of book releases: it's tough to get the word out to the world.

Even if your book has been published by one of the biggest publishers in the country, you—the author—are still expected to do most of the work in letting the world know it's there.

An author might host a book signing at a local bookstore or library. Or might host an online party on Facebook.

More likely, an author will sit at home, staring at the book's Amazon sales ranking and biting her nails.

Instead, why not join up with other authors to support each other?

If several authors have books in print, they might join together for a single book signing, not necessarily at a book's release. Depending on the size of the location, authors could have several tables for their books and have fun together meeting readers and encouraging each other. Even if no one sells a single book, you have networked and encouraged each other. You can later meet and determine if you might have done something different or better. Then you can plan for the next event and make it better.

You can also form up a group of several writers, all of whom expect to release a book within the next year or two. By joining up, you can create excitement for each other's release through guest blog posts, interviews, book reviews when the book releases, and other online cyber launch events.

You can set up ideas for what each member will do for each other member when their book launches. Knowing you have help and support when your book releases, can make all members more enthusiastic about supporting each other. Remember that when we work with other people on their books, we have an element of ownership in that book. We believe in that book and want it to succeed.

That feeling is reciprocated by others who believe in our book.

My Example: Although I have helped other writers with book launches by inviting them to post on my website or interviewing them about their new book, my best example is when others helped me.

I had been writing a series of books on women in Scripture. When I was ready to release my third book, I decided to launch the entire series, basically marketing the series, rather than just the new release. Several other authors (whose books I had also helped market) joined me to create a week-long launch tour.

On Monday, I was interviewed on one friend's website. On Tuesday, Wednesday and Thursday three colleagues posted reviews of my three books on their websites. On Friday, I hosted a *Cyber Book Launch Lunch* on my own website.

At the *Cyber Book Launch Lunch*, I offered downloadable recipes for three dishes I had created—each one referencing one of the three books dedicated to a woman in Scripture. I had a recipe for Eve's Garden Salad, Ruth's Barley Soup and Hamantachen cookies, a traditional Jewish dessert made during the celebration of Purim, instituted by Queen Esther. On that Friday, I also held a drawing for a copy of a book for the readers of each of the other four websites.

Having four other writers help me launch my series was wonderful. Not surprisingly, the experience also encouraged me to seek out ways to return the favor to them and others.

We all need help getting word out about our books, especially at release time. Finding ways to cooperate with each other can be more effective and certainly more fun.

> Book signings and launches can be daunting. Who do you know who might appreciate working together in person or online?

Chapter 20

Miscellaneous Activities

Yes, we write in the corner of a closed office. Ultimately though we must leave that office and let people know about our work. Other writers do too. Think about how you can join up with a few of those other writers—to work together; to write and market better.

Not every person will want to do every marketing activity suggested in this book. But try a few and see what works for you.

Here are a few more ideas. Maybe one of them will get you started brainstorming into even more directions.

- Consider where most of your readers might hang out on social media. If your reader is a young mother, she will likely hang out on Facebook. If your book is a non-fiction book about business practices, your reader might be more likely to be part of Linked-in. Don't try to have a presence on every social media site. Instead, focus your attention where your readers will be.

- Don't forget about Author Central, Goodreads and your Amazon Author page. Although those are not areas on which you can joint market with other authors, you can share links to other author's pages. And they can share your link.

- Provide each writer in your joint marketing group with a short quote about their writing to use in marketing documents, such as press releases.

- Think about ways to teach a class together, either in person or online. Do podcasts together. Have videos and seminars either live or recorded and offer them on each other's websites.

- Hold a joint fundraiser event and advertise that $5.00 (or whatever) from the sale of each book benefits a charity you select. Community fund-raising events are often listed in local newspapers at no cost.

- Gather your group and buy a table at a holiday bazaar.

What can you think of to add?

For everything having to do with marketing, remember the key points:

- All of us hate marketing.

- All of us must market anyway.

- Believe in the value of what you have created.

- Do unto other authors as you would have them do unto you.

What other ideas do you have for joint marketing activities? Who do you know who might be interested in doing them with you?

Part Three:

Mastermind Groups

Chapter 21

What is a Mastermind Group?

Steven Covey first coined the term *Mastermind Group* in his book *The 7 Habits of Highly Effective People* (Simon & Schuster, 1989). Here is a brief summary of those seven habits. Consider how they relate both to life in general and to your writing career specifically.

1. Be proactive.

Stay positive and focus on what you can accomplish. Take responsibility for yourself and what you do.

2. Begin with the end in mind.

Plan what you want to accomplish. Then take action. Keep up to date. Focus on the end. Revisit your goals regularly. Stay accountable.

3. Put first things first.

Determine the order of importance of your goals. Work on them in order of importance.

4. Think Win-Win.

Focus on how everyone can benefit in each situation. Don't ignore other people. Remember that everyone should benefit.

5. Seek first to understand, then to be understood.

Understand the needs of other people before you can be able to help them. Additionally, focus on others first before your own needs.

6. Synergize.

Value each other's differences. That allows groups of people to discover more possibilities. Group ideas are usually better than anything you come up with on your own.

7. Sharpen the saw.

Keep learning individually and together. If you learn something about the craft of writing, critiquing, marketing, achieving goals, motivation or life in general—share that with each other.

A mastermind group is a group of like-minded people who gather together to achieve something important. They succeed because they work together using the above seven habits.

By looking at each of those seven habits as they relate to writing you can understand how a mastermind group might be highly successful in helping each individual member grow in their craft of writing, the quality of their product and in marketing their books.

Of course, a mastermind group will be more productive if there is a unity of purpose and mission for all members. For example, an engineer who wants to launch a new computer software and a woman who wants to open a part-time cleaning business may both think having a mastermind group will benefit them. But having something more in common than a desire for success will enable them to work together better and achieve more.

For you as a writer then, naturally a mastermind group of other writers will be best. Determine further if your group should consist of writers in a single genre or if all members might benefit from multiple genres. At least, settle on a unifying mission for the group, such as to grow individual platforms or to pursue ongoing book publication. By having such a more general mission, you might still then be able to include members who write in a wide variety of genres.

Then find your members. Just as you might find other critique group members or people with whom to joint market, revisit the suggestions in chapters 2 and 10. Seek out like-minded writers committed to a career in writing, committed also to continuing improvement and helping others in the writing community.

After you have a group of possible writers, you might suggest that everyone read Covey's book, *The 7 Habits of Highly Effective People.* It has been in print continuously since 1989. In other words, it's worth reading, especially if you are asking for deep commitment by a group of individuals.

And, since I have no financial interest in Covey's book, hopefully, you understand how that makes my recommendation even more credible. If not, please reread Chapter 12 on Reciprocal Book Reviews.

Once you have received commitment from your individual writers to be part of a mastermind group, it's time to set some guidelines.

A mastermind group is a think tank on steroids. It is powerful because each member of the group taps in to the mind of each other member and the master mind of the group as a whole.

Chapter 22

Determine What Each Member Can Contribute

One of the greatest aspects of a mastermind group is the diversity of its membership. All members may be writers. All members may even write in the same genre. But each member is an individual. Each member has something unique to offer—with background, experience, preferences, knowledge and creativity different from every other member.

First then, it is helpful to determine the strength of each member and how those strengths benefit the whole. You might just begin a discussion. Or if you are left-brained like me, you might create a simple survey.

Ask about their strengths in writing, marketing, editing.

Ask for thoughts about the level of commitment they expect to have for the group.

Ask about time or effort restrictions they might have that limit participation with the group.

Find out what venues they have available to them. Do they regularly write for magazines? Volunteer at a library? Are they part of a homeschool network and could promote your children's books? Just having a website or professional social media page is a resource that can be offered and utilized for the group.

Once you have a group of like-minded and committed writers, you can work to determine how your mastermind group will run.

I created a simple questionnaire you might use when talking with others about setting up a mastermind group. It is little more than a survey. But each member might be surprised at what they have to offer—in addition to how they might personally benefit.

That questionnaire is coming up next.

Focus on how everyone will benefit by determining the needs, skills and resources of each member.

Chapter 23

Mastermind Questionnaire

Here is a sample survey questionnaire you might use to understand the needs of each member and how they might specifically contribute to the group. Use this or create your own, based on the focus of your group.

~+~

- What I write: genre, books, magazine or newspaper articles, blog
- The specific project I am presently writing and my expected release date
- The project I expect to begin next
- What specific online resources I have access to: web; blogsite; social media
- What in-person resources I have access to: bookstore owners; libraries; church groups, book clubs

- What I feel comfortable doing in the area of technology, writing, leadership, marketing, business development, publishing:
- What challenges me most as a writer:
- What I need help with most:

~+~

Look at the individual skills, strengths and resources of each member. A mastermind group does not necessarily need every member to be widely published to be successful. Rather, it is often more important to have members who are committed to the group's purpose, have something of value to offer and a willingness to use it to help other members of the group.

Once you have clarity on the skills, strengths and resources of your group, it is time to settle on the group's structure.

> Every member of your group has a skill, a strength or a resource to offer—even if it is "only" creative ideas. Understanding what they have to offer will help each member participate more fully.

Chapter 24

Mastermind Structure

There are many ways a mastermind group can be run. And all of them are valid. There will generally however be one type of organizational structure that works best for a particular group.

Just like creating a critique group, determining initially how your mastermind group will run will make things work better for the long haul. Here are three ideas for structure.

Horizontal Structure

In this type of group, each member has equal input on everything. There may be a person who initially sets up the group but then relinquishes leadership in favor of every member being equal.

Any questions about writing, group responsibilities or disputes are discussed among all members. Nothing is done behind the scenes. Every person takes full ownership of the group.

This type of group usually runs best if everyone is already familiar with each other and there is both trust and respect among all members.

Vertical Structure

In this type of format, one person is elected leader and has control of the group. Sometimes this makes things easier; sometimes it is problematic.

I was leader for two online critique groups and both groups ran smoothly. Every member knew exactly what was expected of them although I occasionally had to remind folks about our submission schedule or nag someone that another member was waiting for their critique.

I was a member of another online group however where disputes went directly to a leader, outside of the general overall group discussion. She made decisions for the group. Despite her tact and kindness, the lack of discussion about decisions led to the group's breakdown.

The point is that having vertical structure can work or not, depending on the makeup of the group, the rules set in place and the leader's personal leadership style.

Starburst Structure

With the starburst structure, each member has responsibility for a specific task or area based on their ability and desire.

One member might be facilitator of the meetings. Another might be administrator—reminding members of meeting dates and responsibilities committed to. Another member might take minutes. Another member might be the official accountability nag—reminding each member of their goal commitment and keeping them on task to work toward them.

In the starburst structure, each person focuses on their individual skills, resources and how they can best help the group.

In short, there are many ways to structure a mastermind group—one of these or a combination of more than one. Make your mastermind group structure the way it makes most sense for your individual members and as the group as a whole.

How do you envision your mastermind group being run?

Chapter 25

Mastermind Guidelines

After you have determined your mastermind group structure, it's time to set more specific guidelines for how the group will operate.

First, determine how frequently the group will meet and for how long. You might start out with a dedicated time each week to meet in person or online. And settle on a length for the meeting so members will know what to expect and can allow adequate time.

Whether you meet in person or online, you will still need to have online collaboration from time to time. How will that be handled? Via email? A Google Group? How will documents be shared?

Perhaps the most important aspect of mechanics to be determined will be the structure of each meeting. There will need to be adequate time for sharing, advising and accountability for and by each member, without each meeting extending too long.

A reasonable suggestion when a group is starting out is to schedule one-hour weekly meetings. Keep track of time and break down your meeting structure into three sections.

First allow 15 minutes of sharing the writing highs and lows from the past week by each member. Broken down, then, those 15 minutes would allow 3 minutes of sharing by each member of a 5-member mastermind group.

Then the group might have a 30-minute section of advising. On a rotating weekly basis, for example, one member would be on that week's "hot seat." That member would have the chance to express what he is working on and the problems or challenges he is facing. He would then tap into the master mind of the group for help. During this time, other members would make suggestions and come up with creative solutions or actions he might take.

At the end of the meeting, there could then be 15 minutes where each member in turn takes two or three minutes each to commit to one activity they would be held accountable for achieving before the next meeting.

That example of meeting structure would adequately address the three elements of a successful mastermind group: sharing, advising and accountability.

Certainly, each mastermind group should determine the scope of what they will cover and set up a schedule for each meeting to achieve that. To be most efficient, each member should also come to the meeting prepared with what he will express during both the sharing and accountability sections of the meeting.

Structure helps ensure that one person does not monopolize the time during meetings or that other people never have their needs addressed. Remember Covey's seven principles. Number 4 is "win-win." The group should benefit each and every member.

One key to a successful, long-term mastermind group is to respect the needs of all members, allowing adequate time for a productive meeting, while respecting busy lives.

Chapter 26

The Commitment Required

Several years ago, I formally set out to establish a mastermind group of writers. When I approached the other three authors I had in mind, I was surprised that none of them had heard of the term *mastermind group.* Nor had they read Stephen Covey's book, although of course they all had heard of it.

Nonetheless, after I explained what I had in mind, all four of us agreed to participate for one year. The commitment wasn't as enthusiastic as I had expected but I was hopeful they would gain enthusiasm as they began to understand the value of the group. We committed to reciprocal book reviews, discussed marketing, set writing and marketing goals and kept each other accountable for them.

At the end of the year, the group disbanded as planned. Everyone agreed it had been a worthwhile endeavor. But no one was particularly interested in continuing.

The enthusiasm I had hoped for never caught on...because the initial, deep-seated commitment had been absent.

On the other hand, my long-term children's critique group who worked together for over 15 years was essentially a mastermind group, even though we didn't call ourselves that. We helped each other take ideas and develop them into books. We critiqued each other's work and helped with revisions, as well as final copy edits. We shared publisher information about which editors were looking for what and which agents represented what type of work.

We suggested marketing ideas and of course faithfully reviewed each other's books as they were released. We worked together to do public speaking and even presented workshops together. We supported each other's book signing events.

Each January we also announced our writing goals to each other and followed up quarterly to review them and be held accountable for what we said we were going to do.

We called ourselves a critique group; but we were a mastermind group. We had a common purpose. We supported and encouraged each other. We took ownership of the books the other members created. We believed in each other, the books we wrote and the readers for whom we had devoted our writing to.

We shared. We advised. We had accountability.

Maybe you're not ready for a full-fledged, all-encompassing mastermind group. Or maybe that's exactly what you need. Or maybe you are somewhere in between.

Think about how you might look at whatever existing writing group you are part of and take all of you to the next level of working together for the benefit of each other and your readers.

Creating a Mastermind Group requires deep commitment by all members. Fortunately, you don't need many members for one to function well. Do you have a group of 3 or 4 other writers who might be committed to working together in several aspects of writing?

Chapter 27

Working Together; Finding Success

Whether you have a simple critique group, a tight focus group, a general encouragement group or a mastermind group, always be thinking of how to help other writers. If nothing else, even if you don't set up a formal group of any kind, pick an author or two you know. Subscribe to their blog and they to yours; comment on their posts; share their posts or quote each other on social media. When a topic they write about comes up somewhere, say "I know an author who wrote about that." And share that information.

If you set up a formal group, whatever its purpose and scope, it will be more successful if every member starts out with a clear understanding of how it will run.

Any group of writers—critique groups, writing partners, a few folks banding together for marketing or full-fledged, committed mastermind groups—all have the potential to take your writing, marketing skill, career, friendships and personal development beyond whatever you might have imagined doing on your own.

Any of these groups require time. They require commitment. They require effort.

All worthwhile things do.

Whether you start with one writing partner or jump into the deep end with a group of dedicated masterminds, I wish you success in all your writing endeavors.

Remember that although we may sit in the corner of our office with the doors closed, we can also work in community with other writers who are doing the same. The hopeful result is that our books are better for us having worked with each other. And because our books are better, our readers—for whom we do this in the first place—are blessed.

Best wishes to you in your writing career.

Are you ready to get started working with other writers? Who will you approach? What will you suggest doing together first?

Appendix I

Posting Amazon Reviews

Locate the book on Amazon.com. Click on the book title to bring up a new page. Or provide the Amazon URL to take your reader directly to your book page.

Scroll to the bottom of the page to Customer Reviews.

Click the "Write a customer review" button.

Click on the number of stars you would give the book.

Amazon should then ask you how you want to post. If you have posted reviews before, it will suggest the name you used previously. If you have never reviewed books, it will lead you to a screen to create your Amazon reviewer identity. Otherwise first name and last initials work fine, or you can create something clever, like Book Addict or Reading Papa. The review name you create is linked to your Amazon account. So next time you post a review, it will remember you.

If you are an author writing a review for another author, you will want to use your own name so that your name is seen in the book world as much as possible.

Click in the *write review box* and type in your review. The review need not be lengthy or inspiring. It's more important to be honest and encouraging to people who might be looking for just what the book offers.

Enter a title for your review. It could be something as simple as "Great book" or "This book helped me…" Sometimes it's easiest to write a review and then enter a title based on a phrase or key word in your review.

After you've finished your review, click *Preview your review*. The screen will show what your review looks like. If it is OK, click *Publish review*. If you want to make changes, click the white *edit* button, make your changes, review it again and then hit *publish review*.

You will receive notice in the email account linked to your Amazon account when your review goes live.

Appendix II

Author Interview Templates

The first template is for interviewing an author with a new book release.

INTERVIEWER: Thank you for joining us today. Congratulations on the release of your new book, *[insert title]*. In one or two sentences, can you tell us the basis of your new book?

AUTHOR:

INTERVIEWER: What was the most exciting (or memorable) part of writing this book?

AUTHOR:

INTERVIEWER: What was the hardest (or most challenging) part of writing this book?

AUTHOR:

INTERVIEWER: What one thing about this book or about the topic or theme in general would you like readers to know?

AUTHOR:

The following is a general interview focused on writing:

INTERVIEWER: Thank you for joining us, [insert name]. How long have you been writing for publication? What first got you started?

AUTHOR:

INTERVIEWER: Tell us what genres you write. Is that also what you most like to read?

AUTHOR:

INTERVIEWER: Tell us about your latest book.

AUTHOR:

INTERVIEWER: Do you have a work in progress you can tell us about?

AUTHOR:

INTERVIEWER: What's your biggest challenge in writing?

AUTHOR:

INTERVIEWER: What one thing would you like people to know that I haven't asked?

AUTHOR:

INTERVIEWER: Thanks so much for sharing your writing journey with us. We look forward to your future projects!

Author's Thanks

Thank you for reading this book. I hope you read something that will help you find, maintain and grow valuable relationships within the writing community.

You can find me online at my website CarolPetersonAuthor.com. I'd love to hear from you.

If this book was valuable to you as a writer, please consider going to Amazon.com and leaving a review. Remember what I suggested back in Part Two, Chapter 12 (Reciprocal Book Reviews)? I would do it for you, friend.

Best wishes!

Books by Carol Peterson

From Honor Bound Books

Writer's Book Shelf Series

- *The Praying Writer: Prayers & Scripture for the Writing Process*
- *The Write Brand: Becoming Known in the World*
- *Working Together; Achieving Success: Critiquing, Marketing, Masterminds*

With Faith Like Hers Bible Study Series:
Studies on the character and circumstances of women in Scripture. Books available or coming soon:

- *I am Eve*
- *I am Esther*
- *I am Ruth*
- *I am Mary*
- *I am Elizabeth*
- *I am Rahab*
- *I am Hannah*
- *I am Deborah*

Flowers, Gemstones & Jesus: Finding Jesus in the Months of the Year

Mustard Seed Books
(children's imprint of Honor Bound Books:

- *Counting Blessings* (Picture Book)
- *You and Me at the Sea* (Picture Book)
- *Stealing Sunlight* (Middle Grade Novel)

From Libraries Unlimited

- *Fun with Finance: Math + Literacy = $uccess* (2009)
- *Jump into Science: Themed Science Fairs* (2007)
- *Around the World Through Holidays: Cross-Curricular Readers Theatre* (2005)
- *Jump Back in Time: A Living History Resource* (2004)

Made in the USA
Coppell, TX
05 February 2021